W9-DGI-693

Hockey

ice HOCKEY

GETTING THE EDGE: CONDITIONING, INJURIES, AND LEGAL & ILLICIT DRUGS

ice HOCKEY

Hockey

by Gabrielle Vanderhoof

Mason Crest Publishers

HUNTINGTON CITY TOWNSHIP
PUBLIC LIBRARY
255 WEST PARK DRIVE
HUNTINGTON, IN 46750

ice
HOCKEY

Copyright © 2011 by Mason Crest Publishers. All rights reserved. No part of this publication may be reproduced or transmitted in any form or by any means, electronic or mechanical, including photocopying, recording, taping, or any information storage and retrieval system, without permission from the publisher.

MASON CREST PUBLISHERS INC.
370 Reed Road
Broomall, Pennsylvania 19008
(866)MCP-BOOK (toll free)
www.masoncrest.com

First Printing
9 8 7 6 5 4 3 2 1

Library of Congress Cataloging-in-Publication Data

Vanderhoof, Gabrielle.
  Hockey / by Gabrielle Vanderhoof.
    p. cm. — (Getting the edge: conditioning, injuries, and legal & illicit drugs)
  Includes bibliographical references and index.
  ISBN 978-1-4222-1735-1   ISBN (set) 978-1-4222-1728-3
  1. Hockey—Juvenile literature. 2. Hockey—Training—Juvenile literature. I. Title.
  GV848.3.V36 2011
  796.355—dc22
                              2010010054

Produced by Harding House Publishing Service, Inc.
www.hardinghousepages.com
Interior Design by MK Bassett-Harvey.
Cover Design by Torque Advertising + Design.
Printed in the USA by Bang Printing.

The creators of this book have made every effort to provide accurate information, but it should not be used as a substitute for the help and services of trained professionals.

Contents

ice HOCKEY

Introduction

GETTING THE EDGE: CONDITIONING, INJURIES, AND LEGAL & ILLICIT DRUGS is a fourteen-volume series written for young people who are interested in learning about various sports and how to participate in them safely. Each volume examines the history of the sport and the rules of play; it also acts as a guide for prevention and treatment of injuries, and includes instruction on stretching, warming up, and strength training, all of which can help players avoid the most common musculoskeletal injuries. Each volume also includes tips on healthy nutrition for athletes, as well as information on the risks of using performance-enhancing drugs or other illegal substances. GETTING THE EDGE offers ways for readers to healthily and legally improve their performance and gain more enjoyment from playing sports. Young athletes will find these volumes informative and helpful in their pursuit of excellence.

Sports medicine professionals assigned to a sport with which they are not familiar can also benefit from this series. For example, a football athletic trainer may need to provide medical care for a local gymnastics meet. Although the emergency medical principles and action plan would remain the same, the athletic trainer could provide better care for the gymnasts after reading a simple overview of the principles of gymnastics in GETTING THE EDGE.

Although these books offer an overview, they are not intended to be comprehensive in the recognition and management of sports injuries. They should not replace the professional advice of a trainer, doctor, or nutritionist. The text helps the reader appreciate and gain awareness of the sport's history, standard training techniques, common injuries, dietary guidelines,

and the dangers of using drugs to gain an advantage. Reference material and directed readings are provided for those who want to delve further into these subjects.

Written in a direct and easily accessible style, GETTING THE EDGE is an enjoyable series that will help young people learn about sports and sports medicine.

—*Susan Saliba, Ph.D., National Athletic Trainers' Association Education Council*

1
Overview of Hockey

Understanding the Words

Incentive *means reason to want to do something.*

Amateur *refers to sports for which players are not paid.*

Recruiting *is what happens when someone persuades someone else to be a part of a team or other group.*

Agents *are people who represent players and try to get them good-paying positions.*

ICE

Ice hockey—or as it is known in the United States, simply "hockey"—is the world's fastest team sport. Players have been clocked at 29 miles per hour (47 km/h), while the puck speeds at more than 100 miles per hour (160km/h). The game's exciting combination of speed, agility, and power skating has won over thousands of fans.

Although the sport is especially favored in cold climates, it has gained popularity—both more followers and players—since the increase of artificial ice rinks and indoor arenas, the first being built in 1875 in Montreal, Canada.

The History of Hockey

The sport developed from bandy, an English game that is played like hockey, but with simple sticks and a small, hard ball. It was first played in the beginning of the nineteenth century, but too-mild winters caused its popularity to dwindle; it is still played by Scandinavians and Russians today, though.

An international bandy game between Finland and Norway in the 2004 Women's World Championships.

Hurling, an ancient Gaelic sport, is played with sticks and balls on a field. Ice hockey could originally have been a modification of a game like this for a cold, icy climate.

During the winter of 1853, bandy was transformed into the game of hockey. A troop of soldiers stationed in Canada decided to replace the ball with a disk-shaped block of wood for their bandy games played on a frozen lake. And on March 3, 1875, the first indoor hockey game was played, in front of spectators, in Montreal.

W. F. Robertson and R. F. Smith, who were students at McGill University, devised the first set of official rules for the game in 1879. They combined some from rugby and field hockey, added the first rubber puck, and set the number of players on a team (six—a goaltender, two backs, and three forwards.)

One year later, the first-ever hockey club, the McGill University Hockey Club, was formed. Soon after, the sport began to catch the public's interest, and it quickly spread around Canada and the northeastern United States.

Then, in the 1893–1894 season, the Governor General of Canada, Lord Stanley Preston, donated a cup to be given to the leading Canadian hockey club. This sparked incentive and competitiveness within the sport, and amateur teams sprang up throughout the country; the teams began recruiting good athletes to compete for the new Stanley Cup.

In 1887, the Ontario Hockey Associated was established to oversee amateur hockey, and by 1896, the United States had caught on as well—the U.S. Amateur Hockey League was established with four clubs in New York City; the first game ended in a 15–0 victory by the St. Nicholas Skating Club over the Brooklyn Skating Club. Soon, colleges began accepting the game as an important addition to their sports programs and calendars.

Professional Hockey

The next step for the sport was to go professional, and in the early 1900s in Canada, Michigan, and Pennsylvania, it did. The National Hockey Association was founded in Canada in 1909, and three years later, professional teams were competing for the Stanley Cup. In 1917, the National Hockey League (NHL), an outgrowth of the National Hockey Association, was founded in Canada, again with four teams. By 1924, U.S. clubs were added to the NHL, expanding the league to ten teams total.

The sport received an even bigger popularity boost when it was played unofficially at the 1920 Olympic Games in Antwerp, Belgium. (Oddly enough, the games took place during the summer.) The Canadians won the gold, beating three other teams: United States, Czechoslovakia, and Sweden.

When expansions to some rules were made in the late 1920s—the forward pass in all three zones of the ice, for example—hockey became faster-paced and soared in popularity. By 1942, the NHL was narrowed down to six major teams: the Boston Bruins, the Chicago Black Hawks, the Detroit Red

CRESCENT HOCKEY TEAM

An amateur hockey league was established in 1896 in New York City. The team pictured here, the Crescent Hockey Team, were the champions of this league in 1911.

Wings, the Montreal Canadiens, the New York Rangers, and the Toronto Maple Leafs.

Until 1967, these six teams competed for the Prince of Wales Trophy for the league championship, and the top four teams faced off for the Stanley Cup. Soon after 1967, however, the league doubled in size; the original teams became known as the Eastern Division, and the rookie teams represented the Western Division. Expansion has continued nearly each year to reach the thirty teams we see play today. They make up six divisions: Eastern, Western, Central, Atlantic, Northwest, Northeast, Pacific, and Southeast. The four

Gordie Howe (1928-)

Called "Mr. Hockey," Gordie Howe played for five decades (1946–1980). Howe took part in the Detroit Red Wings camp at the age of sixteen, and then played for them as right wing from 1946–1971. Next, he played for the Houston Aeros (1973–1977) alongside his two sons, Mark and Marty, and moved with them to the Hartford (now New England) Whalers (1977–1980). Retiring at age fifty-two, he returned briefly in 1997 at age sixty-nine.

He was the first player to score 1,000 major league points (goals and assists) in a career, ending with 1,850. He set NHL records for the most goals (801), games (1,767), and seasons (26); won the Hart Trophy for the most valuable player six times; and took six scoring titles. Noted for his toughness, he fractured his skull in 1950 and was told not to play again, but he was back the next year as the league's scoring leader.

"You've got to love what you're doing," Howe said. "If you love it, you can overcome any handicap or the soreness of all the aches and pains, and continue to play for a long, long time."

Gordie Howe, pictured here in 1966, is the only hockey player to have played in the National Hockey League over five different decades.

leading teams now have playoffs, which lead to a final best-of-seven game series for the Stanley Cup—the Superbowl of hockey.

Hockey Goes Worldwide

Thanks to Canadian students who were studying in England, hockey was brought to Europe in the first half of the twentieth century. Hockey began to be played in 1902 at the Prince's Skating Club in London, which led to the formation of a league consisting of five teams. The International Ice Hockey Federation (IIHF) was established in 1908, and a year later, field hockey players introduced the game to Czechoslovakia. Bandy players (from Scandinavia

ICE

and Russia) played their first hockey game in Sweden in 1920, in Norway in 1934, and in the Soviet Union in 1946.

Predictably, Canadian teams dominated the early years of Olympic hockey, winning six of the first seven gold medals; Great Britain won the other. Starting in 1956, the Soviet Union became the front-runner, winning its first of seven gold medals. Canada tied this record in 2002 by taking gold, defeating the United States with a score of 5–2. The United States has only won twice—in 1960 and 1980—but each time it was a major upset where they defeated the favored teams with spectacular performances. These games, one

Wayne Gretzky, "The Great One," was one of only six players chosen for the International Ice Hockey Federation's (IIHF) Centennial All-Star Team in a poll conducted by a group of 56 experts from 16 countries.

HOCKEY

Wayne Gretzky (1961-)

Known as the greatest hockey player in history, when Wayne Gretzky retired in 1999 after twenty years in the NHL, he held or shared sixty-one records. He holds the all-time scoring record of 2,857 points, with 894 goals and 1,963 assists in 1,487 career games. The only player in the history of the NHL to score more than 200 points in one season, he led the league in scoring nine times and was named the most valuable player nine times.

Born in Brantford, Ontario, Canada, he began his career in 1978 with the Indianapolis Racers of the World Hockey Association. That same year, he was traded to the Edmonton Oilers, whom he led to four Stanley Cup championships (1984, 1985, 1987, 1988). He was traded to the Los Angeles Kings in 1989, when he became the NHL's highest-ever scorer. In recognition of his achievements, the league has now retired Gretzky's jersey number; number 99 will never again be worn by any NHL player. Gretzky was inducted into the Hockey Hall of Fame seven months after he retired.

known famously as the "Miracle on Ice" led to an upswing in participation by young players throughout the country and greatly expanded the number of hockey fans. The U.S. women's Olympic hockey team also gained fame, winning the first-ever women's competition at the 1998 games in Nagano, Japan, by defeating the Canadians two times, 7–4 and 3–1. The Canadians got their revenge, though, in the 2002 games, defeating the Americans 3–2.

The Hockey Hall of Fame was established in 1943 and completed its own building in 1961 within the Canadian National Exhibition grounds in Toronto. In 1993, it moved to a new $35 million facility in downtown Toronto, drawing more than 500,000 visitors in its first year.

Basic Hockey Rules

Hockey is played on ice by two teams of six players each: a goaltender to protect the goal, a center, left and right wings who skate near their sides of the rink, and left and right defensemen who defend near their goal. The players

High glass barriers that protect fans from stray pucks surround official NHL rinks.

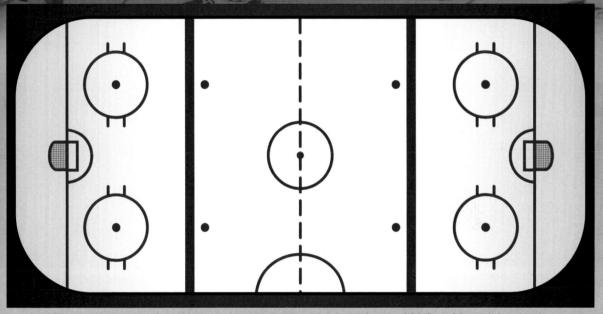

The regulation size for a National Hockey League rink is 85 feet by 200 feet. Most high school and college rinks have adopted this as the standard size for their rinks as well.

skate holding a wooden stick to control and pass the puck, which they shoot at the opponent's goal.

The game lasts for three twenty-minute periods, with a fifteen-minute break between each period. If the game is tied at the end, a five-minute "sudden death" overtime is played, and the first team to score wins.

The Rink

An NHL rink is 85 feet (26 m) wide and 200 feet (61 m) long, and has rounded corners. Surrounding the rink, to protect the fans, are plastic or fiberglass boards 42 inches (1.06 m) high, and there is often shatterproof glass above the boards. Blue lines divide the rink into three sections: the neutral zone in the center; the defending zone, where a team protects its goal; and the attacking zone, the opponent's goal. Face-off circles are also drawn on the ice in nine positions where the puck may be put into play by a referee or linesman.

The Game

The game begins with a face-off in the middle of the rink, with the referee dropping the puck between the opposing centers. Players on the team con-

Hockey games begin with a face-off at center ice. Players face off in order to begin play after a penalty or other violation as well.

It is a violation of the rules of hockey for players to use their stick as a weapon. Doing so can result in time spent in the penalty box.

trolling the puck pass it down the rink and can score by directing it between the posts of their opponent's goal, as long as it completely passes the red goal line in front of the goal. The other team can intercept the puck at any time, and a player can "check" an opponent by making hard body contact with him to stop a pass or shot.

If a player draws a penalty, he must spend time in the penalty box, a bench located just off the ice. Five minutes are assessed for a major penalty, such as fighting or "spearing" (using the stick like a spear against an opponent), and two minutes for a minor one, such as tripping or holding. If a player is illegally denied a scoring opportunity, the referee may award a penalty shot in which that player alone moves the puck from the center toward the goalie, one-on-one.

NATIONAL HOCKEY LEAGUE TEAMS

Eastern Conference	Western Conference
Atlanta Thrashers	Anaheim Mighty Ducks
Boston Bruins	Calgary Flames
Buffalo Sabres	Chicago Blackhawks
Carolina Hurricanes	Colorado Avalanche
Florida Panthers	Columbus Blue Jackets
Montreal Canadiens	Dallas Stars
New Jersey Devils	Detroit Red Wings
New York Islanders	Edmonton Oilers
New York Rangers	Los Angeles Kings
Ottawa Senators	Minnesota Wild
Philadelphia Flyers	Nashville Predators
Pittsburgh Penguins	Phoenix Coyotes
Tampa Bay Lightning	San Jose Sharks
Toronto Maple Leafs	St. Louis Blues
Washington Capitals	Vancouver Canucks

Opportunities to Play Hockey

U.S.A. Hockey Inc., the U.S. governing body for the sport, oversees teams for players aged six and under as well as youth teams, which are divided by age into divisions called Mites, Squirts, Pee Wees, Bantams, and Midgets. All leagues are well organized and must use approved protective equipment and meet certain standards of behavior on the ice.

Training is available at many local hockey schools and camps, including Summer Development Camps sponsored by U.S.A. Hockey, which hosts regional, national, and officiating camps across the country. Acceptance is very competitive.

Many annual championships are also available for players of different ages. The International Youth Hockey Tournaments currently host forty teams in the United States.

THE COLLEGE GAME

Hockey, once confined to the cold climates of Canada and a few northeastern American states, has taken advantage of modern arenas to expand into high schools and colleges throughout the warmer states. The North still dominates the college sport, with six major conferences: the Central Collegiate Hockey Association, Eastern Collegiate Athletic Conference, College Hockey America, Hockey East Association,

Opportunities for young people to play hockey exist at the elementary school, high school, and college levels.

Like Father, Like Son

Bobby Hull (1939–) scored 610 goals in 1063 games in sixteen NHL seasons (1957–1972) as left wing with the Chicago Black Hawks. A Hockey Hall of Famer, he is acknowledged as one of the greats of the game. However, his son Brett bettered that total at right wing, scoring his 611th goal in the first game of the 2000-2001 season with the Dallas Stars and his 700th on February 10, 2003, with the Detroit Red Wings, becoming only the sixth player in NHL history to reach that mark.

Bobby Hull led the NHL in scoring seven times, but his team won the Stanley Cup only once, in 1961. Nicknamed "the Golden Jet" because of his blonde hair, he was known for his fair play, which won him the Lady Byng Trophy for good sportsmanship in 1966. His son, Brett, was nicknamed "the Golden Brett" and was traded to the St. Louis Blues in 1987, scoring 527 goals in his ten seasons there. In 1999, he clinched the Stanley Cup for Dallas in triple overtime against Buffalo, and in 2001, he helped Detroit win the Stanley Cup.

Metro Atlantic Athletic Conference, and Western Collegiate Hockey Association. The NCAA's annual championship comes down to the playoffs of the "Frozen Four" top teams.

The names of NCAA divisional tournament winners form a good list that high school players can study if they wish to continue their game, possibly into the professional ranks. The Division I championship has been won nine

times by the University of Michigan; seven times by the University of Colorado Denver; three times by Lake Superior State University (Michigan), Michigan Technological University, and the University of Minnesota; and twice by Colorado College, Cornell University, the University of Maine, Michigan State University, and Rensselaer Polytechnic Institute (New York). The Division II championship was discontinued in 1999. Its top winners were Bemidji State

Women's ice hockey, added to the winter Olympics in 1998, is one of the fastest growing women's sports. Women are not new to the sport, though—the first recorded game was played in Canada near the end of the 19th century.

University (Minnesota), which won five titles, and the University of Massachu-setts at Lowell, which won three. The most championships won in Division III have been five by Middlebury College (Vermont) and two by Plattsburgh State University (New York). The University of Minnesota at Duluth won the NCAA Women's Championship in 2003 for the third consecutive time.

PLAYING PROFESSIONALLY

Many college players who are not drafted into the NHL have found satisfying careers with minor league hockey teams, and some then move up to the NHL. With most sports, there are leagues that come and go over time, and hockey is no exception to this. The top professional minor league is the American Hockey League, or AHL; this league is currently comprised of twenty-nine teams, and it is where the NHL recruits many of their players. It is generally considered just one step down from the NHL. The ECHL, formerly known as the East Coast Hockey League is another main minor league, and has twenty widespread teams, including the Cincinnati Cyclones, the Las Vegas Wranglers, and the Florida Everblades. Established in 1988, the ECHL has sent 435 former players to the National Hockey League to date.

Many smaller minor leagues, such as the United Hockey League, the Central Hockey League, and the Southern Professional Hockey League also offer opportunities for advancement. Although a player must be eighteen to be picked in the NHL draft, agents have approached some players as young as fourteen, hoping to represent them. Any high school player who signs with an agent, however, becomes ineligible to play at an NCAA college. The NHL draft is held in June each year. Teams that do not make the playoffs have the first selections from the draft, and any expansion clubs are added to this group. The order of draw is selected by a lottery. The teams that made the playoffs then choose players in reverse order, with the last-place team choosing first.

An NHL career can be financially rewarding. For the 2009–10 season, 56 NHL players will receive a salary of at least $5 million. The top-paid player in the league is Vincent Lecavalier, a center for the Tampa Bay Lightning, who earned $10 million in 2010.

But whether you play professionally—or have fun playing in community leagues—the game of hockey is always exciting, challenging, and demanding. That's why it's important to prepare well, so that you're in the best possible shape you can be when you hit the ice.

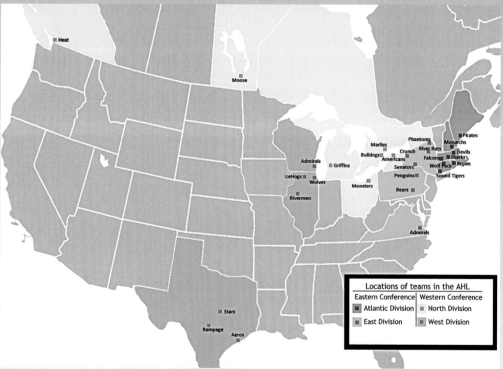

This map shows the distribution of teams currently in the American Hockey League.

Chronology of Hockey

1853

First hockey game played with a disk, which replaced the ball used in bandy.

1879

First rules drawn up by two McGill University students.

1908

The International Ice Hockey Federation (IIHF) established.

1917

National Hockey League (NHL) founded and played its first season.

1920

Hockey played as a demonstration sport at the Olympics.

1923

Hart trophy for the NHL player "most useful to his club" first awarded.

1926

Vezina Trophy for the NHL goaltender allowing the fewest number of goals first awarded.

1930

First World Hockey Championship tournament played.

1936

Calder Memorial Trophy for the NHL's outstanding rookie first awarded.

1943

The Hockey Hall of Fame established in Toronto.

1947

Annual NHL All-Star Game first played; Art Ross Trophy first awarded to NHL's leading scorer.

1967

NHL expands from six to twelve teams.

1981

The Hobey Baker Award for college hockey's Player of the Year first presented.

1990

First Women's World Hockey Championship tournament played.

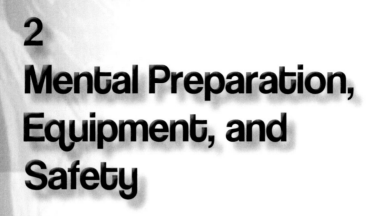

2
Mental Preparation, Equipment, and Safety

Understanding the Words

Enhance *means to make something better, to improve it.*

Receptive *means that someone is willing to listen to and appreciate something.*

Rituals *are acts regularly repeated in a set way.*

Routines *are things that are always done the same way, procedures that have become habits.*

ice HOCKEY

Imagination is a powerful force. We have all experienced the near reality of memory and daydreams, especially during times free from outside distractions. The use of this vivid imagery has become an important technique to help enhance sports performance. Your coaches set physical goals for you and your team to help sharpen your skills on the ice, but you alone are in control of what goes on in your head and your mindset before, during, and after a game.

Hockey players and other athletes have turned positive mental control into a regular program to improve their self-confidence, motivation, and performance. Skills can be reinforced and improved when a player imagines playing at a high level and achieving victory. Sports psychologists call this technique "visualization."

An important benefit of visualization is that it helps build a positive self-image, which is important on the ice. Negative thoughts can cause not only defeat but injuries. When you surround yourself with negative thoughts, you are more likely to experience negative things. Imagine yourself being in control on the ice and doing your best. Remember that your performance is in

Famous Nicknames in Hockey

- Jeff Reese, goalie: "Peanut Butter Boy"
- Dave Shultz, left wing: "The Hammer"
- Sidney Crosby, center: "Sid the Kid"
- Yvn Cournoyer, right wing: "The Roadrunner"
- Bobby Hull, left wing: "Golden Jet"
- Sid Abel, center: "Old Boot Nose"
- Wayne Gretzky, center: "The Great One"

your hands alone, and positive reinforcements will make all the difference in your game.

"Rehearsing" in the Mind

Train your mind regularly, especially during the season, to keep in top mental shape. Spend ten to fifteen minutes a day away from the rink visualizing what you need to focus on to succeed, and then another three to five minutes

The mental aspect of a sport can sometimes be harder to learn than the sport itself. Coaches help players getting physically ready for games, but they also teach players mental preparation.

before a game doing the same thing. A relaxed state makes you more **receptive** to mental imagery. It is obviously easier to relax at home in moments when you can totally concentrate, such as lying in bed before you fall asleep. A short pre-game mental session is also a good idea, and many amateur and professional hockey players practice what is called "relaxed attention," both during the break between periods or while sitting in the penalty box. In this mental state, players

DID YOU KNOW?

A hockey variation for disabled players is sledge hockey. This action occurred between Norway and Japan at the 2002 Winter Paralympics in Salt Lake City, Utah.

This image shows an example of a "screen play." The player in the dark jersey standing in front of the goalie is trying to block his view of the current play.

Tactics and Strategies

The speed of hockey seems almost to defy measured tactics, but the best players can anticipate action down the ice and employ a variety of moves to adjust to the situation and confuse the other team. Some of these moves include:

- **Screening**: Players on the attacking (offensive) team will position themselves in front of the goalie in order to screen or block the goalie's view of an upcoming shot.
- **Deflection shot**: Instead of taking a straight shot at the goal, which may be anticipated by the goalie, an attacking player shoots the puck to a nearby teammate, who quickly deflects it toward the goal from a different angle.
- **Deke move**: Deke is short for "decoy." Here, an attacker fakes the direction of a pass or move by the movement of his or her stick or head and shoulders. Players use many clever "deke" faking movements in order to outmaneuver opponents.
- **Pulling the goalie**: A team can gain an extra offensive player by moving the goalie to join the attack. This is a desperate ploy for a team facing defeat in the last minutes, and it leaves the goal open if the opponents control the puck.

HUNTINGTON CITY TOWNSHIP
PUBLIC LIBRARY
255 WEST PARK DRIVE
HUNTINGTON, IN 46750

ICE

are calm yet energized, so relaxed and confident that their actions on the ice seem to be almost automatic, which makes for less conscious effort and exhaustion during the game.

When visualizing yourself in a game, try to imagine the game as clearly and realistically as possible in your head. See the blur of the jerseys swarming around you, the sound of the blades against the ice, the roar of the crowd, the referee shouting, the crack of the stick on the puck, the thump as an opponent is checked against the boards, even how you will feel under the weight of your own uniform and the stick in your hand. Note your emotions as you speed over the ice, maneuvering past the last defense for a clear shot at the goal—or, if you are the goalie, imagine yourself hunkering down to block a shot.

DID YOU KNOW?

The largest audience ever recorded in a hockey game was on October 6, 2001 between two college rivals, the University of Michigan and Michigan State University. The game is commonly referred to as the Cold War. A $500,000 sheet of ice was used, and there were 74,544 spectators in attendance.

Reinforce your skills by adding mental images of particular movements of your body and keep your mind in check with your body's muscle memory of certain moves. Revive the memories of your best plays, such as your best backhand shot, a perfect assist to a teammate, or strength in your shoulders as you body check your opponent. Focus on the way you felt after an outstanding play and the excitement you heard from the crowd. The more often you focus on success, the more often success will seem "the norm" during a game, and you will work harder toward reaching that goal. By visualizing all these things—sounds, sights, feelings, movements, you will feel more and more comfortable every time you step out onto the ice and the less you'll notice your nervous jitters will be before a game.

HOCKEY

Superstitions

Athletes in almost every sport have their own set of superstitions. There are rituals and routines that each player sticks to before a game. Whether these superstitions actually work like magic is not likely—but what is for sure, though, is that like mental reinforcements and visualization, these rituals can have a huge impact on athletes' performance, good or bad, simply by altering their mental state during a game.

Here is a list of some well-known NHL hockey players, and what they say "works" for them.

Wayne Gretzky

"I never get my hair cut when we're on the road because the last time I did, we lost."

"I always put my equipment on the same way: left shin pad, left stocking, right shin pad, right stocking. Then pants, left skate, right skate, shoulder pads, elbow pads, first the left, then the right; and finally, the jersey, with the right side tucked into my pants."

"During the warm-up, I always shoot my first puck way off to the right of the goal. I go back to the dressing room and drink a Diet Coke, a glass of iced water, a Gatorade, and another Diet Coke."

Patrick Roy

"Before every game, I meticulously lay out each piece of equipment on the locker room floor and I always dress myself in the same order."

"Between periods, I juggle with a puck and bounce it on the ground. Then I put it in a special place where no one will find it and make off with it, otherwise . . . so the legend goes, bad luck could befall the culprit and he would suddenly turn into an alligator."

Hockey Terms

- **Body check**: Using the body to block the puck carrier, stopping an attack on the goal.
- **Changing on the fly**: Substituting players without stopping the game.
- **Clearing the puck**: Shooting the puck away from the front of the goal or out of the defending zone.
- **Face-off**: An action beginning play, when the referee drops the puck between the opposing centers.
- **Hat trick**: Three or more goals scored in one game by the same player
- **Icing**: A rule violation whereby an offensive player shoots the puck from behind the center red line all the way across the opponent's goal line—unless, of course, it scores a goal (the line extends across the rink and the goal itself sits on only a small part of it.)
- **Offsides**: A rule violation whereby an offensive player goes past the blue line into the attacking zone before the puck does.
- **Slap shot**: A hard shot taken by swinging the stick in a long sweeping motion
- **Stick check**. Using the stick to take the puck away from opponents, with a poking, hooking, or sweeping motion

Bob Gainey

"In between periods, I always ask for a drink made with 30 percent Coke and 50 percent water. I've had this habit ever since I started to play for the Canadiens."

Doug Soetaert

"I change my shin pads after every pre-game warm-up."

Jocelyn Thibault

"Before a game, I always lay my equipment out on the floor in the same way and six and a half minutes before the game, I pour water over my head."

Bobby Smith

"I use surgical tape to protect my wrists instead of hockey tape like the other players."

Stéphane Richer

"No. 10 is stamped on all my sticks."

Equipment

Even if you have great skating skills and hockey moves, none of them will do you any good on the ice or in a game if you don't have the right equipment to back them up. It may not seem like a vital part of your performance, but it is important to never skimp on safety, especially in a rough, high-contact sport like hockey.

SKATES

First, the most important piece of equipment is hockey skates. There are many types of skates out there—figure skates, speed skates, and recreational skates that may resemble hockey skates—however, to avoid injuries

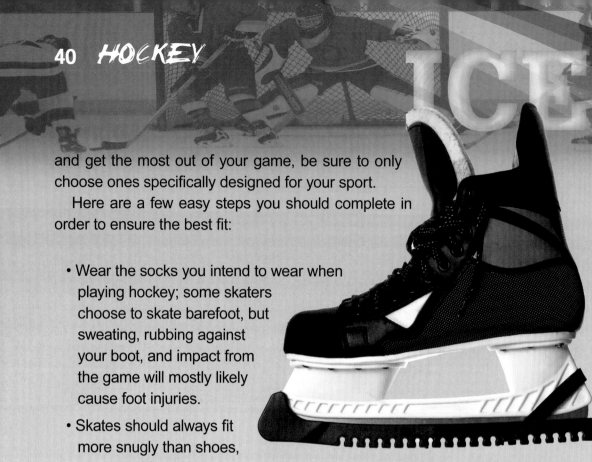

and get the most out of your game, be sure to only choose ones specifically designed for your sport.

Here are a few easy steps you should complete in order to ensure the best fit:

- Wear the socks you intend to wear when playing hockey; some skaters choose to skate barefoot, but sweating, rubbing against your boot, and impact from the game will mostly likely cause foot injuries.

- Skates should always fit more snugly than shoes, so start with a skate one size smaller than your shoe size. Don't count on the fact that you may grow into them, because for the time being, you will have insufficient support for your foot, which can also lead to injuries.

- Tap your heel on the floor a few times to make sure it is set back firmly in the boot.

- Lace the skates firmly for a snug fit.

- Stand with your feet shoulder-width apart and crouch slightly, so that the knee is over the toe. Your foot will shift slightly. This is the "skating stance" for hockey players. If your toes are scrunched up, the skate is too small. If your foot has any room to move inside the boot, the skate is too big. It needs to feel perfectly snug, but not too tight.

PROTECTIVE EQUIPMENT

While skates are the most vital piece of equipment needed in order to play, the rough nature of the game makes protective pieces a close second. When you see a hockey game being played at nearly any level, players are fully covered head-to-toe in protective gear.

Hockey is an enjoyable sport, but there are many dangers on the ice. The hard flying puck, skates with sharp steel blades, the hockey stick's swinging blade and shaft, and collisions on the ice all cause a variety of injuries—and many more are prevented by the high-tech protective equipment worn by amateurs and professionals alike.

Helmet and Mouth Guard

Hockey players at all levels are required to wear a helmet because a hard blow to the head by the puck or a stick could cause a serious injury, including a concussion. It is important that a player makes certain that the helmet

ICE

fits perfectly, both for safety and comfort; it should fit snugly and not wiggle, just as skates should fit your feet. The lightweight plastic helmet is lined with pads, at least 5/8 inch (13mm) thick, to absorb any impact; some models have an extra lining to increase comfort. All have holes on the sides for ventilation. In addition, helmets have either wire facemasks, plastic face shields, or a combination of the two, to guard against injuries to the nose, jaw, teeth, and eyes. The wire versions, often made of stainless steel, cover all the facial area and will not fog up like some face shields. The plastic shields cover the front of the face and offer a better overall view. Many do fog up, but some are now produced with a special coating that resists fogging. A combination face protector is available with a plastic shield to guard the upper part of the face, including the eyes, and a wire mask below to protect the jaw and enable easier breathing. An extra safety item for the helmet is a pair of ear protectors, which also provide warmth.

A mouth guard should be worn to give extra protection to the teeth, and it can also protect against concussions by softening blows to the head. A mouth guard is sold already formed and can then be softened by heat and molded to each individual when the player bites down.

Gloves

Gloves are made from leather, nylon, Kevlar®, or a combination of these materials. Sizes range from 9 inches (23 cm) for youth hockey players to 16 inches (40 cm) for adults. Some players prefer a slightly larger fit for comfort, but the padding should cover both the hand and wrist. Gloves should offer good protection for the thumb, fingers, and wrist, but be soft enough to let

HOCKEY

Wearing proper safety equipment, including helmets, gloves, and pads, is the best way to prevent injuries due to the puck, ice skates, sticks, or collision.

a player feel and grasp the stick. Some players prefer short gloves, but these should be accompanied by wrist guards.

Padding

The hockey uniform is well padded underneath. Shoulder pads protect the shoulders, collarbone, chest, back, and upper arms. An attached part adds rib protection.

Defensemen in the line of fire need larger pads. Additional pads are available to protect the heart area and lower back; they are either part of the shoulder pad or an attachment. Attacking forwards wear lighter pads to offer more freedom of movement. Elbow pads, which can be adjusted with Velcro® straps, should be long enough to cover from the shoulder pad to the glove. These protect against bruises and fractures. Some players add extra protection for their forearms by wearing what is called a forearm slash pad. Shin pads, which cover the kneecap and down to the boot top, are required to guard against being struck by the puck or a stick. Again, defensemen wear heavier pads than forwards.

The Goalie

A goalie is most often in the line of fire, the target of flying puck shots and powerful attackers. This explains why goalies look like astronauts about to step on the moon. Their protective equipment weighs as much as 40 pounds (18 kg) more than that of their teammates. Shin guards are 4 inches (10 cm) thick or more, and are worn outside the socks to cover the leg from the thighs to the ankles. Padding for the shoulders, chest, and arms is also thicker.

The gloves for both hands are distinctive. The one on the hand holding the stick is called the "blocker glove" or "waffle pad" (in the game's early days, goalies used a rectangular pad with holes, which looked like a waffle). It is used to block shots and knock away the puck. The other is the "catching glove," used to scoop up the puck and toss it away from the goal.

Goalies wear more protective gear than any other player because of the risk of injury that they face due to shots on the goal.

Boots are covered with molded plastic for extra protection. More of the boot's blade touches the ice to provide extra security. A goalie can play his best because his equipment takes away most of the worry about serious injuries, letting him play boldly.

Mental preparation and equipment are two important elements of the equation that adds up to safety and success on the hockey rink. The other one is physical training.

3
Physical Preparation

Understanding the Words

Cardiovascular *refers to your heart and blood vessels (cardio = heart, vascular = vessels).*

Aerobic *exercises are those that cause your body to need more oxygen, making your heart and lungs work harder.*

Cartilage *is the rubbery material found between joints, as well as in your nose and ears.*

Strategic *means that something is important to a plan of action.*

Stamina *is strength and energy that keeps going for a long time.*

Hamstrings *are the stretchy bands that attach the muscles to the back of your knee.*

Achilles tendons *attach the muscles of your calves to your heels.*

Your **groin** *is the area where your thighs connect with your body, as well as the area around there.*

Cross training *is participating in more than one sport as a way to stay in shape.*

ice HOCKEY

Warming up before games is a good way to ensure your best performance and avoid injuries. To begin any strenuous physical activity without first warming up your muscles will most likely lead to strained muscles or tendons that will hinder your play. Although it may seem like waste, always allow yourself enough time to warm up before every practice and game.

Stretching

Stretching helps your blood flow and warms the muscles and tendons, loosening and relaxing them. This helps prevent injuries, which happen easily if muscles are tight. A short warm-up also increases your heart rate and pumps more oxygen into your **cardiovascular** system.

Hockey players always warm up before the face-off, but they have less pregame time on the ice than, say, a football player warming up on the field or

These hockey players appear to be suffering from exhaustion, but really they are stretching before a game.

a basketball player on the court. And exercising before coming into the arena is also made difficult because of skates. Even so, short stretching exercises—shoulder shrugs, waist bends, neck turns, knee lifts, and arm circles—can be done on the spot in the locker room before putting on your gear.

Once in the arena, you can continue to stretch while gliding around the ice:

• Bend one knee while keeping the other leg straight behind, then switch to stretch the other leg,

Other exercises while gliding involve using the hockey stick:

• Hold the stick with both hands behind the back and lift it away from the body.

• Raise the stick overhead and tilt the body to the right and left.

• Hold the stick in front and bend forward at the hips.

Cooling Down

You should also take time after a game for a cool-down period, which can be five minutes or less. Hockey is a physically demanding sport that causes the muscles to pump blood to the heart, and these muscles will feel stiff or sore after the game because they will still contain extra blood. Help muscles return more quickly to normal by stretching or walking around the dressing room immediately after coming off the ice. Players who sit down immediately after a game may feel dizzy or even faint.

Daily Exercise

It is important to follow a program of stretching and exercising each day during the season, even when no game or practice is scheduled. This will build up endurance against fatigue, which often leads to injuries. You can maintain flexibility and strength by first stretching to warm up and then doing aerobic exercises, such as running, swimming, push-ups, pull-ups, sit-ups, and jumping jacks. Even if you exercise for only twenty minutes three times a week, this will condition both your legs and upper body. If your fitness level is very good, extend your exercise sessions to an hour. You could also include weight training, but young players should avoid heavy weights, which may injure the cartilage in the body, stunting future growth.

TIPS ON EXERCISING

Any exercise session should take into account a player's fitness, because it takes about six to eight weeks to get into top shape after beginning a conditioning program. Follow these five steps for best results:

1. Start your program gradually, beginning with a workout of about twenty to thirty minutes, which can slowly be increased to an hour. Do not let yourself become fatigued during any session.

2. Warm up before each exercise period by stretching for ten to fifteen minutes first.

3. Exercise to your capacity to build up endurance, but do not overwork your body. If you are breathless and unable to carry on a conversation, reduce the level of intensity.

4. Mix up the exercises to work on flexibility, strength, and the special movements required in hockey—your coach can teach you specific drills specific to your level and position.

5. Establish a daily routine of warm-ups and exercise, both during the season and off-season.

STRETCHING EXERCISES

The following simple exercises could be done in the dressing room before suiting up, but they're also ideal for a daily program away from the rink. Start at the neck and work down. Do each stretch five time and hold for six to ten seconds.

Neck

Lean your head to the right toward your shoulder. Repeat, leaning toward the left shoulder. Interlock your fingers behind your head, and pull your hands gently toward your chest. Grab the back of your head with the right hand, and pull it gently forward to the right. Do the same with your left hand.

Shoulders

Make an exaggerated shrug, moving your shoulders upward with your arms at your sides. Let your shoulders drop and move them in slow circles. Hold

Holding the hockey stick in front of you and bending forward at the waist is a good stretch to do before a hockey game.

your arms out at the sides and try to touch your palms together behind your back.

Back

Lie on your back and grasp your knees, pulling them close to your chest. Lie on your back with your arms spread out on the floor; turn your head to the right, then pull your right knee close to your chest and try to touch it to the floor on the left side. Repeat with the left knee.

Calf and Achilles Tendon

Put your hands flat against a wall and position one foot in front of the other. Move your back leg farther from the wall, pressing the heel on the floor. Switch legs and repeat.

Stand 1 foot (30 cm) from the wall with one leg behind you, keeping both feet flat on the floor. Lean into the wall while keeping your back straight. Switch legs and repeat.

Hamstrings

Stand about 1 foot (30 cm) from a wall and place your hands at shoulder height against the wall. Push against the wall with your back straight, then step back with your right leg, pressing the heel on the floor. Repeat for left leg.

Try this alternative hamstring stretch: sit on the ground with both legs in front. Bend the right knee and keep the right leg flat on the floor until the sole of the foot rests against the inside of your left knee. Then bend forward with your back straight. Repeat for left leg.

How to Train for Ice Hockey

What is unique about hockey is the wide array of skills that a player must master. It is impossible to become a top athlete in this sport if you are a specialist in only one area of play. Hockey combines puck handling, skating, passing, shooting, as well as the physical contact side of the game, like checking an opponent. You not only need to be tough but quick on your feet, ready to make an important decision at a moment's notice. That is why hockey is not only a physical sport, but a mental and strategic one, as well.

A good ice hockey training program should address each component of the game equally to ensure that its players are well rounded. Strength training, such as running drills to increase stamina, is split into two types: on-ice drills and off-ice drills, also called dry-land training. The former is usually

The hamstring muscles are the large muscles at the back of the thighs. They can be stretched in a seated position, as shown, or by standing and leaning against a wall.

ICE

done during pre-season and the regular season, and the latter is done during the off-season.

Skating speed is one of the most important aspects of hockey, where again, you need to be quick on your feet in order to stay right on the puck and your opponents. You can improve your speed on the ice through interval sprints and simply practicing with other players in order to develop your quickness and reaction time with the stick and puck during the craziness of a game.

Box lacrosse is an indoor version of lacrosse. Some ice hockey players play box lacrosse during their off-season to stay fit.

By training off the ice you can improve your flexibility and muscle mass in the most important areas of the body for hockey. These areas include the hamstrings and Achilles tendons, groin muscles, and the upper leg muscles. Squats, lunges, cycling, and leg presses will help you strengthen these areas, which improves speed and stamina, as well as reduces injuries. Remember, though, never start any training program alone without a certified trainer, coach, or doctor recommending what you should do.

The goalie's training is slightly different than that of other hockey players. He or she will not need nearly as much stamina and endurance training, but instead, a coach will tend to focus solely on the goalie's quick reflexes, lots of stretching to avoid muscle strains that can occur while blocking a shot, and physical strength. (Goalies are wearing up to 50 pounds of protective equipment at a time!)

Although you should practice your hockey skills as much as possible, cross training can also be especially effective. Because hockey requires excellent motor skills, it can't hurt to take up another sport at the recreational level, just for fun. For example, golf, tennis, racquetball—all these require precise hand-eye coordination, patience, and skill. Many European hockey players have used soccer to cross train since the 1950s and 1960s, and a number of Canadian players play box lacrosse during their off-season.

No matter how much you prepare, both mentally and physically, however, injuries do happen sometimes. When they do, the proper treatment and recovery procedures will help get you back on the ice as quickly as possible.

4
Common Injuries, Treatment, and Recovery

Understanding the Words

Contusions *are bruises.*

Lacerations *are scrapes or cuts.*

Something that is **acute** *is very serious.*

Traumatic *has to do with something that seriously harms or shocks the body.*

A **tendon** *is the stretchy tissue that connects your muscles to your bones.*

Repetitive *means that something happens over and over.*

Ligaments *are the stretchy bands that connect muscles to muscles.*

Compression *is the act of squeezing something.*

Elevation *is the act of raising or lifting something.*

Circulation *is the blood flow within your vessels.*

Mobility *is the ability to move easily.*

Rehabilitation *is the process of getting something back to its normal, healthy state.*

Pelvic *has to do with the area between your hip bones.*

A **hematoma** *is a pocket of swelling that is filled with blood.*

Neuropsychological *refers to an area of psychology that focuses on brain function. Neuropsychological tests are designed to examine a variety of thinking abilities, including speed of information processing, attention, memory, and language. By testing a range of these abilities and examining patterns of performance in different areas of thinking, neuropsychologists can gather clues as to whether the brain is functioning normally or if it has been injured.*

ice HOCKEY

Hockey is a hard-hitting collision sport. Players regularly hit the ice and boards, or are hit by the speeding puck, swinging sticks, and even their opponents. Fighting can break out among players, especially at the professional level. The assumption is that with all that protective equipment, there's no risk for injury. However, this offers a false sense of security; you should always know what your risks are, how to avoid them, and most important, how to treat injuries once they occur.

The most frequent injuries in hockey are contusions and lacerations. The latter occur more often to the head and face, despite the use of helmets and face

Hockey is a fast-paced, aggressive, and sometimes violent sport. It is also played on a slippery surface with wooden sticks and a puck flying around. All of these factors combine to create an environment in which falls and collisions are common and so are injuries.

protectors. Muscle injuries are also common because hockey players must twist and turn constantly during games, keeping their balance on thin skates while putting huge amounts of stress on the upper thigh, knee, and abdomen. Upper-body injuries to the head, shoulders, arms, and hands are generally caused by falls and checking against the boards. Some estimates say that illegal plays causes one-third of all injuries. About 80 percent of all injuries in hockey are caused by various forceful impacts on the body, referred to as acute, acute traumatic, or direct-trauma injuries. Believe it or not, being hit by the puck can cause broken bones.

Overuse injury can also occur in hockey. This happens when a player, over time, repeats the same motions over and over, overworking a particular muscle or muscle group. Fatigue can also play a part in overuse injuries. For example, tendonitis, which is the inflammation of a tendon in an area like the knee or shoulder, can be caused by overuse and fatigue. An overuse injury is not as urgent or serious as an acute one (such as a broken bone or cut on the head), but players should seek a doctor's advice to ensure that it does not become worse as the season continues. As difficult as it may be, if a doctor recommends you rest, it's always best to follow instructions to ensure the best possible recovery.

Foot and Ankle Injuries

Even the slightest foot problems can be critical for a hockey player. This includes blisters that result from breaking in new boots. Bones in the foot and ankle can be fractured when hit by the puck or a stick, while ankle sprains result from quick turns at high speeds.

Blisters are an irritating and painful problem that most athletes experience at one time or another. Caused by the boot rubbing against the foot, they generally form on the back of the heel, under the ball of the foot, or on the toes. Blisters often occur at the start of a season when your body is just

One Team's Injuries

To develop strategies for injury prevention, a research group at the University of Michigan Medical School in Ann Arbor studied the injuries suffered by twenty-two members of a Junior A hockey team ages sixteen to twenty. They published their conclusion in the **Clinical Journal of Sports Medicine**:

- Goaltenders had the fewest injuries and forwards had the most.
- The face accounted for most injuries, nearly 24 percent; next came shoulder, hand, and finger injuries, and finally knee and thigh injuries.
- Nearly 80 percent of injuries were contact injuries, including player collisions, stick and skate injuries, board, ice, and puck contact, and fights.
- Players had more than twenty times as many injuries during games as during practices.
- Injuries happened more often in the later periods of games and during the latter part of each period—evidence that fatigue plays a role in causing injuries.
- The injury rate in the first half of the season was more than double that of the second half—implying that players became better conditioned with time and experience.

getting used to frequent wear-and-tear again, but a player should try a new and better fitting boot if blisters occur regularly. Treatment generally involves a doughnut-shaped pad around the blister to cushion the area and prevent further friction, a bandage, and over-the-counter ointments. A blister should be kept clean to avoid infection when it breaks.

Foot fractures—broken bones—are common because a hockey player's feet receive many types of hits. Stress fractures are tiny cracks along a bone's surface, and are caused by repetitive stress on the foot. The main symptom is pain, which increases as use continues. If a fracture is suspected, a player should immediately see a physician to have X-rays done. The only real cure is rest, which requires sitting out a few games. The good news is that young players typically heal faster than adults.

Ankle sprains, which are caused by overstretching the ligaments on the outside of the ankle, are accompanied by pain and swelling. The immediate treatment is to follow the R.I.C.E. program; the letters stand for "Rest, Ice, Compression, and Elevation."

As ankle sprains often recur, the rest period is important and may last from one to six weeks, depending on the seriousness of the tear. It's vital that you rest until you are completely healed; returning to the game too soon will bring the injury back, often worse than before. Ice will relieve the pain and swelling; it should be applied for about twenty minutes at a time and repeated every two hours. If necessary, continue for seventy-two hours. An easy method is to put crushed ice in a plastic bag and then wrap it in a towel, as the ice should not directly touch the skin. Compression means wrapping the ankle with an elastic bandage, making sure that it does not restrict circulation. A team trainer or physician will be knowledgeable about taping and may even decide on a brace to avoid reinjuring the body. Elevating the ankle above the heart level will also reduce swelling.

After about three days, the ankle can be soaked in warm water for about fifteen minutes at a time to help restore mobility. Rehabilitation for the ankle can begin with a light jog, then building up to a normal run.

Leg Injuries

Hockey players often injure their legs during collisions with other players or the goal posts, boards, and ice. The lower leg takes most of the blows from the puck, and additional injuries come from the sticks and skates. These include bruises, muscle strains, and fractures.

Bruises, or contusions, on the leg or other area of the body can rupture small blood vessels, causing blood to pool on the inside of the bruised muscle. The prime area for bruising is the quadriceps (or quads), the large muscle at the front of the thigh. The standard treatment to reduce soreness and swelling is the R.I.C.E. program, especially raising the leg to reduce a further collection of blood.

Muscle strains, also called pulls, are a stretch or tear in a muscle. They're often the result of constant twisting and turning at high speeds. Pulls often occur in the legs, the abdomen, and the pelvic areas. Sometimes they will be caused by a player not warming up enough or by being fatigued late in the game.

Strains and tears generally happen low in the quads and high in the hamstrings, the three muscles at the back of the thigh. For these injuries, follow the R.I.C.E. program, and do light stretching exercises after three or four days, because this reduces the formation of scar tissue. The period of rest from hockey will be four weeks or longer.

Fractures of the leg are rare but serious, as they can end a player's season. They normally occur from a fall or violent collision, and are accompanied by a sharp pain and severe swelling. The most endangered bones are in the lower leg: the large tibia—or shinbone—and the thin, outer fibula. Stress

Fun Facts

- The first hockey puck was wooden, and the first rubber puck was square.
- Although the British did not catch on to hockey until much later than North America did, they are the ones who invented artificial ice rinks, where the ice is frozen electrically.
- The Montreal Canadiens have won the most Stanley Cups in history: 23.
- The original Stanley Cup was only 7 inches (about 18 cm) tall. Today, the cup and its base stand more than 35 inches (about 89 cm) high. The names of every player from the winning team are engraved onto the base of the cup each year.
- The first goalie to ever wear a mask was Montreal's Jacque Plante after a shot broke his nose in 1959. At first he was made fun of for wearing the mask, but now it is a requirement for all goalies.
- The longest winning streak in NHL history is seventeen games, which was achieved by the Pittsburgh Penguins in the 1992–93 season.

fractures from overuse are also common and will feel more like a generalized pain. It is best not to move the broken leg until medical help arrives, but a cold pack can be used to lessen the pain. Obviously, a broken leg must then be treated immediately by the physician, who will take X-rays and decide if a cast, splints, or crutches are needed. Again, the best treatment is always rest.

Knee Injuries

Knee injuries are frequent in hockey, due to a player's turns and falls. Possible injuries include tendonitis, sprains and strains, cartilage injuries, and a dislocated kneecap. Severe knee injuries can even shorten a career.

Knee sprains happen when one or more ligaments become overstretched or torn. In hockey, this is usually the medial collateral ligament (M.C.L.), which is injured when a blow pushes the knee inward. If this happens, you will hear a popping sound and feel deep pain. A strain is a partial or full tear of a muscle or tendon, and this has about the same feeling of discomfort as a sprain. For both, the R.I.C.E. program and several weeks of rest can be combined with the use of a splint or crutches. A knee sprain often requires surgery, especially if the player is a professional or is considering a career in hockey.

A cartilage injury to the knee involves the softer material between bones. Young players are more likely to suffer from this injury. A hard blow to the knee, often from a fall or collision, injures the cartilage, some of which breaks away from the knee bone (patella) and causes swelling and pain. The knee will also lock, and the leg cannot be extended. About 30 percent of these injuries heal themselves over time, but more often than not, surgery is needed; follow up the surgery with exercises like bike riding to strengthen the knee muscles and get them back in shape.

The kneecap, or patella, is the bone at the front of the knee inside the tendon that joins the quadriceps to the top of the tibia, or lower leg bone. A dislocated kneecap can occur when the knee is hit from the front or inside of the knee, or when a player turns quickly and twists the thigh. These accidents knock the moveable kneecap sideways. The area will swell and be painful,

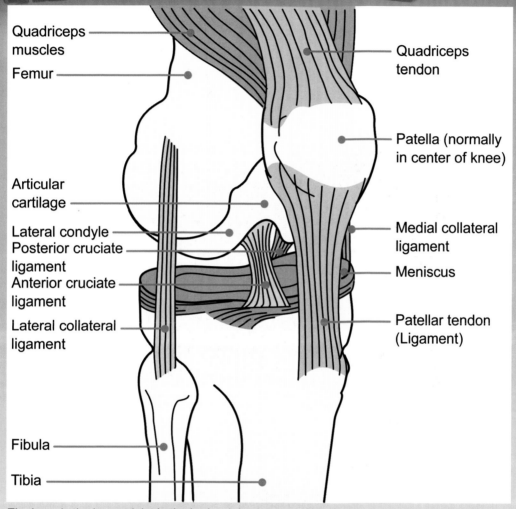

Quadriceps muscles

Femur

Articular cartilage

Lateral condyle

Posterior cruciate ligament

Anterior cruciate ligament

Lateral collateral ligament

Fibula

Tibia

Quadriceps tendon

Patella (normally in center of knee)

Medial collateral ligament

Meniscus

Patellar tendon (Ligament)

The knee is the largest joint in the body—it is also one of the most commonly injured. In ice hockey, knee-to-knee collisions are the most common cause of serious injuries, followed by awkward twisting of the joint due to quick direction changes.

ICE

and the side of the knee usually develops a bulge. The R.I.C.E. treatment is used to treat this injury, and a physician may reset the kneecap (put it back in place) and recommend that the player wear a special brace.

Shoulder Injuries

Shoulder injuries are usually the result of overuse or hard blows (checks against the boards). A hockey player can suffer from shoulder tendonitis, caused by constantly hitting the puck. Separated and dislocated shoulders are the most common injuries.

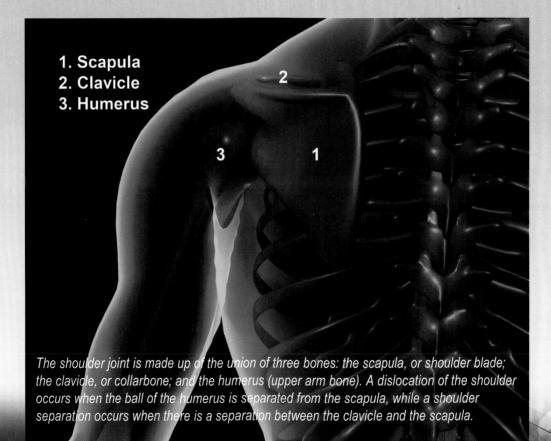

1. Scapula
2. Clavicle
3. Humerus

The shoulder joint is made up of the union of three bones: the scapula, or shoulder blade; the clavicle, or collarbone; and the humerus (upper arm bone). A dislocation of the shoulder occurs when the ball of the humerus is separated from the scapula, while a shoulder separation occurs when there is a separation between the clavicle and the scapula.

A separated shoulder involves the acromioclavicular (A.C.) joint, where the collarbone—or clavicle—joins the shoulder blade. Ligaments keep the joint together, but a blow can tear them, causing the collarbone to rise slightly. This is a painful injury. Most separations are treated with ice packs and healed by rest and strengthening exercises, but a very serious separation might require a physician to wire the joint together.

A dislocated shoulder is more serious because the head of the humerus—the bone that extends from your shoulder to your elbow—pops out of its socket, usually toward the front. This is often caused by a fall or blow directly on the point of the shoulder, which tears cartilage. A doctor will take X-rays, control the pain with medication, and may recommend wearing a shoulder sling for up to three weeks. Surgery is required for only the most serious dislocations.

Hand Injuries

The hands, wrists, and fingers of a hockey player can suffer normal fractures, stress fractures, and sprains. Although falls are the main cause, many times these injuries occur when players remove their gloves to take part in a fight on the ice. The injured parts should be taped with a splint by a trainer or doctor. Or you could just stick to your game and avoid fights all together!

Head and Face Injuries

Most lacerations (cuts) on the head and face can be bandaged and otherwise treated by a trainer with very little lost playing time. A concussion, however, is a head injury that can be a serious matter requiring special attention.

A concussion may result from a hard fall on the ice. In most cases, the injury will be fairly mild, and the player will suffer from a headache, light-headedness, poor balance, and a lack of alertness. Sometimes a player may have

The Miracle on Ice

"It may just be the single most indelible moment in all of U.S. sports history." This is how **Sports Illustrated** describes the "Miracle on Ice" that took place at the Winter Olympics at Lake Placid, New York, on February 22, 1980. The underdogs, the Americans, were going up against the USSR, a seemingly unbeatable powerhouse of a team. Although the Soviets were ahead throughout almost the entire game, American Mike Eruzione shot the puck past the goalie, making the score 4–3, United States.

The game went down in history as the "Miracle On Ice," and just a year later it was immortalized by the release of the movie with the same name, telling its unbelievable story. To this day, the victory is known across the country and the players are still revered.

slight amnesia or even be unconscious for a short period. If this happens, the player should stop playing immediately. Never underestimate such a head injury; a hard blow can possibly create pressure and bleeding under the skull, which can develop into a fatal hematoma. A physician will take X-rays and scans, and the player will have to rest from hockey for a period of a week to a month after the symptoms disappear. The NHL uses neuropsychological testing to ensure that players who suffered from concussions do not return to the ice while still at risk.

Neck Injuries

Minor neck injuries include sprains or strains, such as whiplash, in which the neck is snapped back during play, or "stingers," where the nerves of the neck are stretched, causing a stinging pain and temporary numbness. An injury as serious as a neck fracture may involve the spinal cord, and can result in paralysis or even death. For this reason, an injured player on the ground who has a suspected neck injury should not be moved until an emergency crew arrives. This rule also applies to an unconscious player, who might have both a head and neck injury. Most cases, however, are not severe and require only a rest from the game and a possible neck brace until the muscles are strengthened by exercise.

Returning to Play

One of the most frustrating things about an injury is having to sit out games while recovering. Almost any injury from a sprained ankle to a concussion may recur if a hockey player returns to the ice sooner than recommended. The rehabilitation period may be from several weeks to six months.

Always follow the physician's advice as to medication or physical aids, and pay attention to her directions regarding an exercise program or physical therapy, as well as her recommendations on adjusting your level of play and wearing protective devices. Even after a full rehabilitation period, a player may find that the injured area begins to hurt again during a game. If so, the player should leave the ice immediately and tell both the coach and physician.

Good nutrition can play an important role in an injured player's healing. Sometimes, good nutrition can even prevent injuries from happening in the first place. It's yet another way to give you the edge you want on the ice.

5
Nutrition &
Supplements

Understanding the Words

A **nutritionist** is someone who specializes in helping people eat healthy diets.

Moderation means in the middle—not too much, not too little.

Synthesis means the process of putting something together.

If something is **fortified**, it has been made stronger. When it comes to foods, this usually means that they have had vitamins or other nutrients added to them.

ICE

Although practice and training are an important part of being safe and successful in hockey, you also need to think about what you take into your body in terms of food. Athletes must be careful to eat a proper blend of nutrients to make sure their bodies and minds perform as well as they possibly can. This doesn't just mean eating healthy foods, but also choosing when to eat, how much to eat, and whether or not to take dietary supplements. Of course, when you choose a new diet or supplements, you should consult with a nutritionist, doctor, or some other expert. In other words, do not try to create your own nutrition program.

Fun Facts

- The first ever NHL goalie to score a goal was Ron Hextall of the Philadelphia Flyers against the Boston Bruins in 1987. There was 1:12 remaining and Philadelphia was losing 4–2. The shot traveled the length of the rink and went into the net.
- Henri Richard of the NHL holds the record for most Stanley Cups: 17, in 1956, '57, '58, '59, '60, '65, '66, '68, '69, '71 and '73.
- Dave Schultz holds the record for the most penalty minutes in one season: 472.
- Bobby Orr was the first hockey player to receive the **Sports Illustrated** "Sportsman of the Year" award.

What to Eat

While a balanced diet is important for everyone, it is even more important for athletes. Typically, an athlete has to eat considerably more than other people do. The United States Food and Drug Administration (FDA) suggests that the average American should aim to consume about 2,000 calories a day; for a male high school or college-level athlete, between 2,500–3,000 is more realistic. There are three main food groups to consider when choosing a diet: carbohydrates, protein, and fats.

Daily caloric requirements depend on your age, sex, and activity level. Athletes, in general, need more calories per day than non-athletes.

Gender	Age	Activity Level		
		Sedentary	Moderately Active	Active
Child	2–3	1,000	1,000–1,400	1,000–1,400
Female	4–8	1,200	1,400–1,600	1,400–1,800
	9–13	1,600	1,600–2,000	1,800–2,200
	14–18	1,800	2,000	2,400
	19–30	2,000	2,000–2,200	2,400
	31–50	1,800	2,000	2,200
	51+	1,600	1,800	2,000–2,200
Male	4–8	1,400	1,400–1,600	1,600–2,000
	9–13	1,800	1,800–2,200	2,000–2,600
	14–18	2,200	2,400–2,800	2,800–3,200
	19–30	2,400	2,600–2,800	3,000
	31–50	2,200	2,400–2,600	2,800–3,000
	51+	2,000	2,200–2,400	2,400–2,800

Cholesterol

A lot of bad things have been said about cholesterol—but most of this bad press is focused on LDLs, or low-density lipoproteins, which are a kind of cholesterol that can clog our blood vessels and make our heart work harder. Our bodies make this cholesterol out of saturated fates, like those found in animal fat from meats, butter, and whole milk. However, it is important to be able to distinguish the good from the bad types. The good, HDLs, or high-density lipoproteins, can have a good effect on the body, and increasing your HDL levels can be as easy as exercising regularly.

CARBOHYDRATES

Carbohydrates, or carbs, are foods rich in a chemical called starch, which is what the body breaks down to get energy. Starchy foods include breads and grains, potatoes, cereal, pasta, and rice. Roughly half an athlete's calories should come from carbohydrates, but you should beware of heavily processed carbs, like sugary foods and white bread made with bleached flour. These foods are quickly broken down into sugars, which the body then processes into fats if it does not immediately burn them off. The best carbohydrate choices for an athlete are pasta and whole-grain foods, as well as starchy vegetables, which include vitamins as well as carbs. A balanced diet avoids too many "empty calories" supplied by white bread and sugars.

PROTEIN

Proteins are important chemicals found in all living things; these chemicals are used to perform specific functions inside our body cells. Each protein is a long, folded chain-like molecule made-up of "links" called amino acids. Our bodies can break down proteins that are found in foods into their base amino acids and use them to build new proteins that make up our muscles and bones. For this reason, during any exercise regimen, it is important to eat enough protein to give the body the building blocks it needs to become stronger. The best sources of protein are meats and dairy products, such as milk or cheese, as well as eggs and certain vegetables, like soy, beans and rice.) A good rule of thumb to follow to know how much protein to eat is as

This chart, from the food pyramid at MyPyramid.gov, offers dietary advice for a 2,000-calorie diet. Go to the website to find more personalized and useful information on calorie requirements and healthy diet choices.

GRAINS Make half your grains whole	VEGETABLES Vary your veggies	FRUITS Focus on fruits	MILK Get your calcium-rich foods	MEAT & BEANS Go lean with protein
Eat at least 3 oz. of whole-grain cereals, breads, crackers, rice, or pasta every day 1 oz. is about 1 slice of bread, about 1 cup of breakfast cereal, or ¹/₂ cup of cooked rice, cereal, or pasta	Eat more dark-green veggies like broccoli, spinach, and other dark leafy greens Eat more orange vegetables like carrots and sweetpotatoes Eat more dry beans and peas like pinto beans, kidney beans, and lentils	Eat a variety of fruit Choose fresh, frozen, canned, or dried fruit Go easy on fruit juices	Go low-fat or fat-free when you choose milk, yogurt, and other milk products If you don't or can't consume milk, choose lactose-free products or other calcium sources such as fortified foods and beverages	Choose low-fat or lean meats and poultry Bake it, broil it, or grill it Vary your protein routine — choose more fish, beans, peas, nuts, and seeds

For a 2,000-calorie diet, you need the amounts below from each food group. To find the amounts that are right for you, go to MyPyramid.gov.

Eat 6 oz. every day	Eat 2¹/₂ cups every day	Eat 2 cups every day	Get 3 cups every day; for kids aged 2 to 8, it's 2	Eat 5¹/₂ oz. every day

Find your balance between food and physical activity

- Be sure to stay within your daily calorie needs.
- Be physically active for at least 30 minutes most days of the week.
- About 60 minutes a day of physical activity may be needed to prevent weight gain.
- For sustaining weight loss, at least 60 to 90 minutes a day of physical activity may be required.
- Children and teenagers should be physically active for 60 minutes every day, or most days.

Know the limits on fats, sugars, and salt (sodium)

- Make most of your fat sources from fish, nuts, and vegetable oils.
- Limit solid fats like butter, margarine, shortening, and lard, as well as foods that contain these.
- Check the Nutrition Facts label to keep saturated fats, *trans* fats, and sodium low.
- Choose food and beverages low in added sugars. Added sugars contribute calories with few, if any, nutrients.

follows: the number of grams should be equal to about one-third of your body weight in pounds. For example, a 200-pound person should eat about 70 grams of protein every day, or a 120-pound person should have roughly 40 grams of protein.

FATS

Lots of times, we think of fats as bad for us, since eating too much of them is unhealthy. Despite this negative connotation, fat is an important ingredient needed to make our bodies work correctly. Without fats, our bodies cannot absorb certain vitamins sufficiently. Also, our skin and hair need some amount of fat in order to grow correctly. However, fats should still be eaten in moderation—no more than 70 grams per day. The best sources of fat are vegetable oils, olive oil, and nuts, such as almonds. Many foods contain

What Are Vitamins and Minerals?

Along with carbohydrates, fats, and proteins, you also need vitamins and minerals to make your body work the way it should. Vitamins and minerals are often found in fruit and vegetables. Plants and animals make vitamins, but minerals come from the soil and water, and they are then absorbed by plants through their roots or eaten by animals. If you don't get enough vitamins and minerals in your diet, you may need to take a supplement.

Vitamins and minerals help you fight off infection. Vitamins and minerals also help your body heal more quickly after an injury.

saturated fats, which lead to the formation of cholesterol and can force your heart to work harder.

Dietary Supplements

Many athletes, including hockey players, seek to improve their performance by taking dietary supplements—pills or drinks that contain nutrients or chemicals—to improve their physical health or performance in the game. Dietary supplements do not include illegal performance-enhancing drugs. Instead, they contain vitamins and minerals, and sometimes chemicals that help the body use vitamins more efficiently. When properly used, supplements can improve overall health and performance; but you should always consult a doctor before taking them. Some examples of common supplements include vitamin tablets, creatine, and protein shakes or powders.

Fat-soluble vitamins—A, D, E, and K—dissolve in fat and can be stored in your body. Water-soluble vitamins—C and the B-complex vitamins—need to dissolve in water before your body can absorb them. Your body can't store water-soluble vitamins, so you need a fresh supply every day.

Vitamin	Sources
A (retinol; carotenes)	milk, eggs; carrots, and spinach
B1 (thiamine)	wheat germ, whole wheat, peas, beans, fish, peanuts, and meats
B2 (riboflavin)	milk cheese, leafy green vegetables, liver, soybeans, yeast,and almonds
B3 (niacin)	beets, beef liver, pork, turkey, chicken, veal, fish, salmon, swordfish, tuna, sunflower seeds, and peanuts
C	citrus fruits: oranges, grapefruits, and lemons
D	produced by human body as a result of sun exposure
E	vegetable oils, nuts, green leafy vegetables, and fortified cereals
K	kale, collard greens, spinach, turnip greens, brussel sprouts, and vegetable oils
Folic Acid	broccoli, peas, asparagus, spinahc, green leafy vegetables, fresh fruit, liver, and yeast
B12	meat, fish, eggs, and milk
B6 (pyridoxine)	cereals, yeast, liver, and fish

Drinking enough water is important for all young adults, but athletes especially need to keep hydrated during training and competition. Sports beverages can also help replace minerals and salts that are lost in sweat.

Staying Hydrated

The best diet in the world will do you no good if you become dehydrated. Dehydration occurs when your body doesn't have enough water, leading to fatigue, dizziness, and headaches, all of which can hurt your performance during a game or practice. It is best to carry a bottle of water with you during the day before a game to make sure that you are fully hydrated. In addition, you should be drinking water throughout the game to avoid becoming dehydrated as you sweat. Staying fully hydrated has many benefits besides helping your performance in the game—it can help concentration, improve digestive health, and reduce the risk of kidney stones.

VITAMIN TABLETS

For many reasons, we do not always get the vitamins and nutrients we need. Often because our diets are not as balanced as they should be. Sometimes, it is because the foods that are available to us have been processed so much that they lose their nutrients. Also, exhausted soil all over the country means that fruits and vegetables are often not as nutrient-rich as they could be. In cases like these that are beyond our control, we can get the vitamins we need through supplements. These supplements, which are usually taken in pill form, sometimes contain a balanced mixture of vitamins and minerals (known as a multivitamin), and sometimes they contain a single vitamin or mineral that is lacking in our diet. It is possible to overdose on certain

Hockey and Alcohol

After a big victory, players may be tempted to celebrate with alcohol. They may also be tempted to use it to ease the pain of defeat. But alcohol intake can interfere with the body's recovery process, which may, in turn, interfere with your next game's performance.

It is especially important to avoid any alcohol 24 hours after exercise if you have any soft tissue injuries or bruises. Alcohol and injuries are a bad combination—it can actually increase swelling and bleeding, and even delay the healing process.

vitamins, however, so be careful when taking any type of supplements. More is not always better, so always talk to your doctor before beginning a supplement of any kind.

CREATINE

Creatine is a specific protein that is naturally found in your body's muscle cells. When taken in larger doses than is found in the body, creatine has the effect of increasing the rate of protein synthesis within the body's cells. This means that you will have more energy to exercise, and you will see a greater improvement in strength and speed when you do exercise. Remember, though, that putting any chemical into your system can have negative effects, as well. Everybody reacts differently to different things, so you should talk to a doctor before starting creatine. What's more, creatine is only suited for adult athletes, so young people (those under the age of 17) should not take it.

PROTEIN SUPPLEMENTS

Getting enough protein from the food you can eat can be difficult. Eating protein immediately after a workout is recommended (in order to refuel your body), but most people don't feel up to cooking or preparing themselves a meal immediately after a workout; that's why protein shakes are often a convenient choice. Many shakes contain blends of protein, carbohydrates, and fats, and some include vitamins, to help balance an athlete's diet. Furthermore, having protein immediately after a workout can help repair the damage sustained by your muscles during the workout. You should remember though, that while protein shakes are useful for supplementing your diet, they should not used regularly to replace a balanced meal. You can get plenty of nutrients from a healthy, balanced diet that cannot be replaced by artificial protein shakes, regardless of how fortified they may be. A nutritionist can tell you how to fit protein or supplement shakes into your diet safely and effectively.

With care, supplements can be a healthy part of your nutrition. Other substances, however, such as performance-enhancing drugs, may seem as though they might be a good idea—but they actually cause far more harm than good.

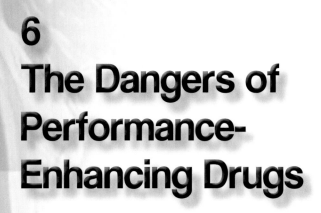

6
The Dangers of Performance-Enhancing Drugs

Understanding the Words

Something that is **debilitating** *makes you weaker or damages your health.*

To **stimulate** *means to encourage something to happen.*

Diuretics *are drugs that make your body get rid of water through your urine. Doing this will make you temporarily weigh less.*

Stimulants *are drugs that speed up your body's processes.*

For many professional players, the pressure to perform well is intense. Hockey players, like many athletes, face stress from everyone around them to constantly improve their skill, strength, and speed. The temptation to use some form of performance-enhancing drug can be all-too real and powerful.

What Are Drugs?

In general, a drug is anything that you place into your body that changes your body's chemistry in some way. Drugs can be useful or beneficial, such as the tablets you might take when you have a headache or antibiotics developed to fight diseases. Steroids are drugs useful for certain people with **debilitating** conditions that cause their muscles to waste away, and steroids can also be used to decrease inflammation. However, many drugs, including anabolic steroids, can have serious negative effects on your health.

Steroids

The most common performance enhancers are anabolic steroids. These chemicals are similar to testosterone, which is the male hormone naturally produced by the body to help **stimulate** muscle growth. That's why when a player takes anabolic steroids, he receives a boost to his speed and strength that is greater than what the body could normally produce on its own. Although the use of steroids is not particularly prevalent in the game of hockey, it does occur every so often. Just as in any high-contact, fast-paced sport, players feel the pressure to step up their game, especially if they are fighting to keep a spot on a college team or trying to maintain a professional career.

Steroids can cause many unwelcome side effects in young male athletes. Some side effects seen in women who take steroids include a deepened voice, increase in facial and body hair, reduced breast size and menstrual problems.

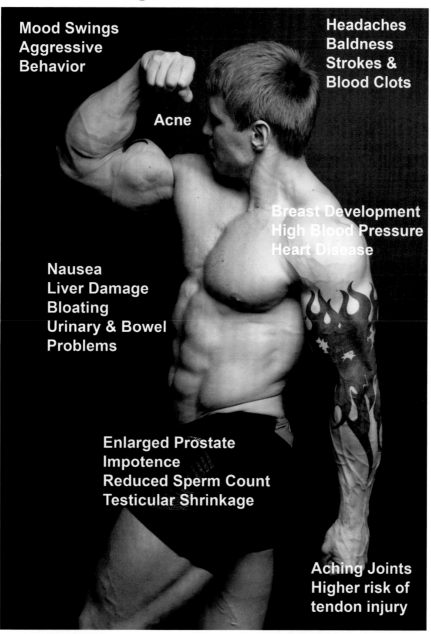

The pituitary gland in the brain releases growth hormone, which stimulates growth of muscle, bones, and other body tissues during especially childhood.

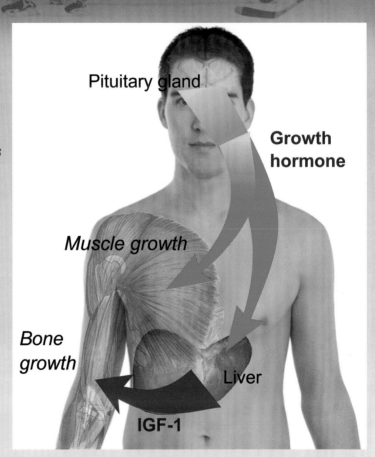

Pituitary gland

Growth hormone

Muscle growth

Bone growth

Liver

IGF-1

Ben Johnson, Canadian Olympic sprinter; Barry Bonds of the San Francisco Giants; and Floyd Landis, winner of the 2006 Tour de France. What do these three athletes have in common? First, they are all three amazing athletes. Second, all three used performance-enhancing drugs. And last, the reputations and careers of all three were forever tarnished.

Landis had his title stripped from him and was dismissed from his cycling team after a urine test came back positive for high amounts of testosterone. Johnson, who won the 1987 World Championships and the 1988 Summer

Olympics, was stripped of his gold medal just days after winning because he tested positive for anabolic steroids; and Bonds was indicted by the federal grand jury and charged with supplying steroids to other athletes.

Steroids can cause an unhealthy increase in cholesterol levels and an increase in blood pressure. This stresses the heart, and leads to an increased risk of heart disease. Large doses of steroids can also lead to liver failure, and they have a negative effect on blood sugar levels, sometimes causing problems similar to diabetes.

If an adolescent (typically someone under the age of about 17) takes anabolic steroids, the risks are often much worse. Steroids stop bones from growing, which results in stunted growth. In addition, the risks to the liver and heart are much greater, since a young person's liver and heart are not fully matured and are more susceptible to the damage that steroids can cause. Furthermore, taking steroids puts you at a greater risk of psychological problems that generally begin with aggression but often lead to much more serious issues. Considering these health risks, as well as the fact that anabolic steroids are almost universally banned from organized sports, they should not be used, except by those who have legitimate medical conditions that require their use.

Human Growth Hormone

Another drug used by some athletes is human growth hormone, or HGH. This chemical is released naturally in the brain when a person is young to tell the rest of the body to grow. However, if an adult takes HGH, it can artificially increase his rate of muscle growth. If someone who has not finished growing takes HGH artificially, it will replace the HGH that is naturally produced by the brain—and when he stops taking it, his brain does not begin producing it again, stunting his growth. People who take HGH also have increased risk of psychological issues.

Illicit Drugs

Sometimes, professional athletes use other drugs unrelated to boosting performance, such as amphetamines and cocaine. The drugs' side effects will usually decrease performance on the ice, so most professional hockey players don't use illegal drugs.

What Are the Consequences of Drug Use?

A positive drug test in professional hockey (the NHL) is not tolerated and has severe consequences for those that do not comply with the rules. For the first positive test, a twenty-game suspension is instated without pay, and the player is referred to the NHL Substance Abuse & Behavioral Health Program for evaluation. For the second positive test, a sixty-game suspension, also without pay, is put in place. And for a third and final offense, the player is permanently suspended from the league, and is only eligible to apply for reinstatement after two years, which must be reviewed extensively by NHL officials.

On the college level, the NCAA sponsors two drug-testing programs, which are both required for every institution part of the association. Athletes are tested during NCAA Championships as well as randomly throughout the year. College athletes are forbidden to take steroids, as well as a variety of other drugs, including hormones, diuretics, stimulants, and any and all street drugs. In fact, the NCAA's list of banned drugs includes more substances than those that are illegal according to federal law. If a NCAA athlete tests positive for a drug test, the student is banned from competing in any intercollegiate sport for an entire academic year, and he loses one of his four years of eligibility. On the second offense, however, the athlete is banned indefinitely from all NCAA sports with no exceptions.

What Professional Players Have to Say About Steroids

Dave Morissette, former **NHLer** and steroid user: "Steroids didn't help me. They didn't make me a better hockey player."

"I had injuries . . . all kinds of surgeries. I wouldn't have had all the injuries without steroids."

Eric Cairns, NHLer: "You just can't be bulky and be a hockey player."

Lawrence Taylor, NFLer: "Steroids are for guys who want to cheat opponents."

Hockey legend Wayne Gretzky once said, "You miss 100 percent of the shots you never take." In other words, if you're too scared, too lazy, or too busy to give something a shot, you'll never know if you could have succeeded. It works that way in hockey—and it works that way in life. Another quote that inspires hockey players is this one, attributed to Liane Carlos: "Continuous effort . . . is the key to unlocking your potential."

Dare to give yourself that edge. Give it your best shot. And then keep trying.

Further Reading

Bahr, Roald, and Lars Engebretsen. *Sports Injury Prevention (Olympic Handbook of Sports Medicine)*. Chichester, UK: Blackwell Publishing, 2009.

Gamble, Paul. *Strength and Conditioning for Team Sports: Sport-Specific Physical Preparation for High Performance*. New York, N.Y.: Routledge, 2010.

Harari, P.J. and Dave Ominsky. *Ice Hockey Made Simple: A Spectator's Guide (4th Edition)*. Manhattan Beach, CA: First Base Sports, 2002.

Price, Robert. *The Ultimate Guide to Weight Training for Hockey.* Sportsworkout.com, 2005.

Smith, Michael A. *Hockey Drill Book: 200 Drills for Player and Team Development.* Buffalo, N.Y.: Firefly Books Ltd., 2009.

Twist, Peter. *Complete Conditioning for Hockey.* Champaign, Ill.: Human Kinetics, 2007.

Find Out More on the Internet

About.com
Weight Training for Ice Hockey
weighttraining.about.com/od/weighttrainingforsport/a/hockey.htm

American Academy of Orthopaedic Surgeons
Hockey Injury Prevention
orthoinfo.aaos.org/topic.cfm?topic=A00114

Ice Hockey Training
ice-hockey-training.com

National Hockey League
www.nhl.com

Sports Injury Clinic
www.sportsinjuryclinic.net

Disclaimer

The websites listed on this page were active at the time of publication. The publisher is not responsible for websites that have changed their address or discontinued operation since the date of publication. The publisher will review and update the websites upon each reprint.

Bibliography

About.com, "The AHL and Other Minor League Hockey," proicehockey. about.com/od/minorleagues/The_AHL_and_Other_Minor_League_Hockey. htm (3 March 2010).

About.com, "How To Properly Fit a Hockey Skate," proicehockey.about.com/ od/learnthegame/ht/hockeyskate-fit.htm (24 February 2010).

BrainyQuote, "Steroids Quotes," www.brainyquote.com/quotes/keywords/ steroids.html (1 March 2010).

CBS Sports, "Highest-paid Players," www.cbssports.com/nhl/ story/10400632 (3 March 2010).

East Coast Hockey League, "Alumni," www.echl.com/alumni/ (3 March 2010).

The Ice Block, "Steroids and the NHL," www.theiceblock.com/hockey/entry/ steroids-and-the-nhl/ (1 March 2010).

Mad About Hockey, "Superstitions," www.mcq.org/societe/hockey/pages/ aasuperstitions_2.html (24 February 2010).

National Collegiate Athletic Association, " NCAA Drug Testing Program," www.ncaa.org/wps/portal/ncaahome?WCM_GLOBAL_CONTEXT=/ncaa/ ncaa/legislation+and+governance/eligibility+and+recruiting/drug+testing/ drug_testing.html (1 March 2010).

National Hockey League Players' Association, "Drug Testing Program Summary," www.nhlpa.com/About-Us/Drug-Testing-Program-Summary/ (1 March 2010).

National Hockey League, "Teams," www.nhl.com/ice/teams.htm#?nav-tms-main (24 February 2010).

New England Sports Network, "Mike Cammalleri, Ryan Miller Fondly Recall Their First Cold War Hockey Game," www.nesn.com/2009/12/mike-cammalleri-ryan-miller-fondly-recall-their-first-cold-war-hockey-game.html (3 March 2010).

Nutty About Sports, "Hockey Trivia," www.nuttyaboutsports.com/sports-trivia/trivia-archive-hockey.shtml (24 February 2010).

_____, "SOME FUN FACTS ABOUT HOCKEY…" www.wannabet.org/Issue/7/hockey_facts.htm (24 February 2010).

USA Hockey, "Summer Development Camps," www.usahockey.com/Template_Usahockey.aspx?NAV=OF&id=230234 (3 March 2010).

World of Sports Science, "Ice Hockey Strength and Training Exercises," www.faqs.org/sports-science/Ha-Ja/Ice-Hockey-Strength-and-Training-Exercises.html (1 March 2010).

Index

Picture Credits

Creative Commons Attribution 3.0 License
    Arnie Lee: pg. 15
    battlecreekcvb: pg. 78
    CillanXC: pg. 16
    Dan4th: pg. 48, 51
    Davidgsteadman: pg. 58
    zappowbang: pg. 33

Creative Commons Attribution-ShareAlike 2.0 Generic
    bulliver: pg. 34

Fotolia.com:
    Andrei vishnyakov: pg.85

GNU Free Documentation License, Version 1.2
    Sean an Scuab: pg. 11

United States Navy
    Matthew C. Haws: pg. 53

To the best knowledge of the publisher, all images not specifically credited are in the public domain. If any image has been inadvertently uncredited, please notify Harding House Publishing Service, 220 Front Street, Vestal, New York 13850, so that credit can be given in future printings.

About the Author and the Consultants

Gabrielle Vanderhoof is a former competitive figure skater. She now works in publishing and public relations. This is her first time writing for Mason Crest.

Susan Saliba, Ph.D., is a senior associate athletic trainer and a clinical instructor at the University of Virginia in Charlottesville, Virginia. A certified athletic trainer and licensed physical therapist, Dr. Saliba provides sports medicine care, including prevention, treatment, and rehabilitation for the varsity athletes at the university. Dr. Saliba is a member of the national Athletic Trainers' Association Educational Executive Committee and its Clinical Education Committee.

Eric Small, M.D., a Harvard-trained sports medicine physician, is a nationally recognized expert in the field of sports injuries, nutritional supplements, and weight management programs. He is author of *Kids & Sports* (2002) and is Assistant Clinical professor of pediatrics, Orthopedics, and Rehabilitation Medicine at Mount Sinai School of Medicine in New York. He is also Director of the Sports Medicine Center for Young Athletes at Blythedale Children's Hospital in Valhalla, New York. Dr. Small has served on the American Academy of Pediatrics Committee on Sports Medicine, where he develops national policy regarding children's medical issues and sports.